How To Find Your Soulmate

A Fundamental Handbook For Discovering Your Soulmate, The Ideal Companion For Your Aspirations

(Discovering Your Ideal Partner And Cultivating A Long-Lasting Bond)

Charlie Murphy

TABLE OF CONTENT

Develop A Comprehensive Understanding Of Their Character And Background. 1

Verbal Communication 16

Desirable Characteristics In Women Appreciated By Men 39

Utilizing The Principle Of Attraction 47

What Are The Attributes That Women Find Appealing? 53

He Is Not Seeking A Companion For Play; Rather, He Seeks A Partner To Assist Him. 61

Online Dating For Women 74

The Fundamental Truth Underlying The Principle Of The Law Of Attraction 84

How To Set And Maintain Appropriate Boundaries 110

Recognize Yourself. 110

Develop A Comprehensive Understanding Of Their Character And Background.

Having a deep understanding of someone is crucial in discerning the precise methods to encourage their romantic affections. Demonstrate your curiosity by inquiring extensively. An integral aspect of cultivating romantic affection involves acquainting oneself with an individual's deepest, innermost aspects and mutually intertwining one's existence with theirs.

Dating and relationships entail the process of establishing connections with individuals, thus entailing a reciprocal effort in understanding and getting to know one another.

However, people, like everything else, are subject to constant change. Over the course of time, it is not infrequent for individuals to rekindle their enthusiasm for a particular skill or activity, or alternatively, to completely forsake it.

Therefore, you must work at better understanding them.

Engaging in substantial dialogue is unparalleled in establishing a profound connection with them. Do not hesitate to inquire about significant matters from them; refrain from solely focusing on your own self. Demonstrate a genuine willingness to delve into their thoughts profoundly and establish an unprecedented level of connection.

CHAPTER TWO

SECRET OF TRUE LOVE

True love is amazing. True love is mystical–Right? Well, sort of. However, this statement holds greater significance, as anyone involved in a romantic partnership could affirm. Acquire knowledge regarding the key elements associated with authentic love by perusing an article on the subject.

1. Genuine love does not involve the act of finding one's own identity within someone else.

Refrain from developing romantic attachments or assuming feelings of love solely with the intention of self-discovery. Your individuality should not be defined by being someone's significant other; it should be defined by being true to yourself. Avoid becoming so engulfed in your relationship that you lose sight of your own identity. There is no requirement for you to possess the status of being the primary admirer of their preferred musical group or peruse each literary material they engage with. Maintain your personal pursuits and engagements, and you will cultivate a greater sense of curiosity and fascination towards your spouse.

2. The most superior approach to uncover genuine love is through the practice of self-love.
It appears to be a commonly used phrase, something often imparted by maternal figures or close friends during periods of emotional distress, but its validity cannot be dismissed–one must prioritize self-love before extending love

to others. Develop a sense of self-assurance and composure, even in the midst of a challenging day. Gain a profound understanding of your true self and ascertain your life goals and aspirations. Cultivating a sense of self-love and effectively managing one's life are not only inherently fulfilling, but also highly sought-after qualities in a potential partner.

3. Authentic love does not impose requirements.
It is imperative that your partner refrains from pressuring you to change when they truly love you. If one sincerely loves their partner, they ought not to anticipate any alteration in their character or behavior. You entered into a romantic partnership based on mutual love and subsequently developed a profound appreciation for each other's unique qualities. What motivation could possibly exist for modifying an individual whom you hold such profound affection for? Embrace

individuals for who they are, and you shall be granted reciprocal regard.

4. Authentic love empowers you to embrace your true self.

Initially, displaying one's true nature in the presence of one's spouse may evoke a sense of apprehension. Waking up with an absence of cosmetics and disheveled hair? What if he were to witness you in the state of being unwell - with symptoms such as a runny nose, bloodshot eyes, and various other manifestations? It is advisable to minimize the occurrence of such a situation for as long as possible. However, it is not advisable for you to harbor such sentiments. In the realm of affection, even the most severe ailment becomes an enchanting encounter, for its value outweighs the adverse impact. The support of your spouse during a challenging situation or their affectionate gestures despite morning breath serve as significant indications of their deep affection for you, signifying a significant stride forward in your journey together.

5. True love comes naturally.
Do you harbor any reservations about your partner? Do you harbor any doubts regarding their suitability for you? If an individual finds themselves grappling with an excessive amount of inquiries concerning their spouse, their relationship, and the prospect of their future together, it is likely an indication that love is not present. In a state of profound affection, one does not harbor doubt or scrutiny. Being in the company of your spouse appears inherently harmonious, and you possess the confidence to overcome any obstacles in order to achieve the envisioned future.

6. In order to acquire affection, one must proffer affection.
It is not possible to cultivate a truly affectionate relationship if one refrains from fully investing oneself. Love cannot be utilized as a bargaining tool. Love should not be employed as a means of

negotiation. The use of love as a bargaining instrument is not permissible. It is advisable to refrain from expressing your love for your boyfriend immediately following his admirable actions within the household. Please refrain from treating him with indifference or aloofness in the event of an error. One must cherish him consistently, irrespective of his words or actions, as sincere affection is boundless. If you extend such a profound level of affection to your romantic partner, you will undoubtedly experience reciprocation, far exceeding your expectations.

7. Genuine love is built upon a foundation of friendship.
Numerous television show collaborations are founded on the gradual development of romantic relationships between close friends. It is an aesthetically appealing concept and a delightful whimsy; however, the actuality does not align with televised portrayals. A profound and lasting love

does not necessitate a lifelong friendship originating from early childhood. However, it is imperative to cultivate a cherished bond of friendship with one's life partner. You must possess the ability to engage in conversation, share laughter, and derive pleasure from one another's presence. Over the course of time, the physical attraction may diminish, yet genuine comrades will endure eternally.

8. True love lasts.
Reflect upon past instances of informal relationships, wherein the mere act of your partner using your bath towel to wipe their nasal mucus was sufficient grounds for termination. The aforementioned relationships lack emotional development, and whatever perceptions you held were not indicative of genuine love. When one experiences authentic love, these occurrences are merely minor obstacles along the journey. No difficulty appears insurmountable. You display a strong willingness to address any challenges,

solely with the aim of preserving our togetherness.

9. True love is devoted.
It is inherent in human behavior to be attracted to fellow individuals, to be captivated by the beauty of a passerby and allow oneself to be affected. Do not allow this to engender feelings of guilt. If one remains steadfastly committed to their spouse, their relationship shall endure. When one is sincerely experiencing love, there is no desire to be in the company of any other individuals. You are unable to comprehend the notion of spending your time without your beloved.

10. You, yourself, are the embodiment of love in your own life.
It is imperative that you bear in mind the essentiality of nurturing self-affection. Self-love is vital, but it's not something you should attain and then put away once you're with your spouse. It is imperative to maintain a profound sense

of self-appreciation throughout the entirety of one's lifetime. If one begins to develop a disdain for oneself or the pursued activities, it becomes necessary to make suitable modifications in order to stay aligned with one's path, maintain a sense of self-loyalty, and preserve a genuine affection towards oneself.

RULES OF TRUE LOVE

Many individuals often enter into relationships without possessing a clear understanding of their own desires and the expectations of their partners. If one desires to have a gratifying partnership, it would be advantageous to acquire a firm understanding of the fundamental principles governing relationships. Regrettably, many relationships unravel following the initial excitement, subsequently causing distress for the couple. A partnership without a vision will lead you nowhere. Therefore, it is imperative to establish and uphold proper standards in order to cultivate a strong interpersonal connection. In this publication, we delve into the fundamental principles that facilitate the cultivation of a wholesome and enduring relationship.

Seventh day: Valuable advice, strategies, and exceptional rebuttals

We extend our heartfelt congratulations to you on the successful culmination of our comprehensive seven-day program dedicated to achieving triumph in the realm of online dating. By ensuring that your profile is optimized for the ideal match, you are establishing a solid foundation for encountering the suitable individual for various social interactions and beyond.

Provided herein are additional pieces of advice and recommendations to aid you in navigating the realm of online dating.

Photographs convey a plethora of meanings and narratives.

Having obtained the profile, ensure that your photograph is suitably fitting. Please refrain from sharing images that depict torsos or provocative poses in the vicinity of the crotch area. Ladies, venture out independently and part ways with the companions who might divert attention from you in your photographs.

Head and shoulder portraits are the most favorable choice among all dating site photographs. If you have the opportunity to include multiple photographs, you have the freedom to experiment with providing full-body shots, as well as incorporating a couple of lively poses or visually captivating images. However, most importantly, ensure that your face is visible in your default photo.

Ask Open-Ended Questions

Regardless of who initiates contact initially or replies to a message, after an exchange of personal inquiries, it becomes necessary to sustain the conversation.

Refrain from asking queries that elicit simple affirmative or negative responses, as such questions tend to hinder the flow of conversation and impede its progression. Instead, inquire about topics that elicit an emotive reaction (preferably positive!) or necessitate contemplation. In the event that they provide concise replies or fail to meet the desired level of responsiveness, it is advisable to redirect your attention towards alternative potential matches.

Encounter Excellence, Discard mediocrity

It is strongly advisable to meet an individual only after experiencing a sense of comfort, but it is prudent to utilize your mobile device and other resources to thoroughly assess potential candidates beforehand.

I am unable to express the frequency of my disappointments upon meeting individuals prior to acquainting myself with them. If an individual coerces you into an early meeting, it is highly likely that they have ulterior motives which are not in alignment with your best interests. Allocate sufficient time to ensure that their qualities align with the criteria specified in your ideal partner profile, and ensure that you give due consideration to the lists that were crafted on the third day. If any of those characteristics surface, it is advisable to exercise caution and maintain a safe distance.

ADDITIONAL RESOURCE: Six Valuable Recommendations for Enhancing Your Online Dating Experience

Don't Give Up

Do you recall the information I previously shared regarding the fact that a notable 10 percent of individuals engaging in online dating tend to discontinue their efforts within the initial three months? As the proverbial wisdom goes, love is a gradual process that necessitates patience. Do not let the negative experiences of the past deter you from rightfully pursuing your feelings. Peruse the profiles and communicate with numerous potential matches by sending messages. Engage in online networking and I am confident that ultimately you will secure a favorable opportunity. Just don't give up!

Verbal Communication

During a conversation between two individuals, particularly in the context of flirtation, they exhibit a heightened level of awareness with regards to each other's behaviors and actions. Indeed, effective communication is nourished by verbal affirmations, constructive cues, and ongoing reinforcement. Do you not experience a heightened sense of satisfaction when the individual with whom you are engaging in conversation responds to your statements?

Regardless of whether this individual utters a single word ("Yes!") or expresses themselves through a complete sentence, their attentive state can be discerned by their verbal reaction. The individual's lack of interruption demonstrates genuine attentiveness to your stream of consciousness. Conversely, an individual who consistently interjects during a conversation demonstrates a lack of regard for others.

An individual who responds using curt, terse language instead of slower and more elaborative speech conveys their lack of interest to the interlocutor. It is not solely the verbiage employed, but also the modulation of one's voice that betrays their degree of engagement. The lack of warmth in one's vocal tone can instill uncertainty in an individual's thoughts.

In the realm of female dating, it is often conventionally advised that women adopt the strategy of appearing elusive. However, it is observed that certain women interpret this guidance excessively literally, deliberately compromising their conversational aptitude by adopting a detached or disinterested demeanor. This arrogant demeanor is what ultimately deters numerous amicable individuals from initiating interactions with women. Ensure that when you verbally respond to a new acquaintance, you project positive signals. Displaying amiability should not be mistaken for an obligation... it was formerly regarded as a courteous gesture that reflects an intrinsic charm that has a captivating effect on men.

Non-Verbal Communication
The act of two individuals engaging in non-verbal communication is commonly characterized by its involuntary nature. Indeed, you might be unaware of the positive or negative cues you are inadvertently emitting in response to someone's communication.

Certain gestures and actions exhibit explicitness and are effortlessly comprehensible. Do you not experience an enhanced sense of relief when the individual with whom you are conversing demonstrates comprehension through affirmatory nods? Do you not experience a greater sense of ease when imparting information in the presence of an individual who actively listens and engages in sustained eye contact? Nevertheless, it is evident that the loss of the person's interest becomes apparent when the audience engages in staring, avoiding eye contact, or exhibiting facial expressions of discomfort.

What is the significance of this in shaping initial perceptions? Given the significance of effective verbal and non-verbal communication, it is imperative that you possess awareness in this domain. Having an understanding of an individual's non-verbal cues facilitates the discernment of their emotional state, thereby furnishing valuable insights on how to guide the discourse. Unquestionably, if an individual of interest averts their gaze or exhibits a yawn during a conversation regarding a former romantic partner, it unequivocally suggests that the narrative is not engaging them.

Not all forms of nonverbal communication are as conspicuous.

Certain gestures can be rather understated. Have you observed behaviors such as self-grooming, crossed arms, or interlocking hands? These movements typically indicate a sense of unease or overall discomfort.

In addition to assisting you in interpreting the nonverbal cues of others, the acquisition of the skill of reading body language will facilitate your consciousness of your own inherent gestures and enable you to exercise self-restraint when warranted. Certain women may find it necessary to exercise control over their involuntary gestures, with consideration for the impressions they might impart upon newly formed acquaintances.

Suppressing an agitated gesture could potentially enhance your prospects of making a favorable initial impression. Certain gestures that are particularly concerning are:

• Proximity that is excessive to the point of encroaching upon personal space during conversation

• Encroaching upon personal boundaries

• Crossing one's arms

• Averting one's gaze from another individual's eyes • Diverting the eyes from the gaze of another person • Refraining from making direct eye contact with someone

• Gently placing your hand on your head or gently massaging your temples

• Sporting an abnormally wide smile or bursting into laughter without any apparent cause.

• Wearing a solemn or impassive expression

One may remain unaware of these involuntary movements until they discern that the individual they are conversing with is physically distancing themselves. When one begins to exhibit signs of apprehension, this sense of unease rapidly permeates throughout those present. Therefore, exercising self-restraint and regulating one's enthusiasm might become imperative.

Exhibiting excessive assertiveness or enthusiasm may inadvertently intimidate certain individuals of the male gender. Typically, men feel a sense of flattery and privilege upon engaging in a conversation with a woman deemed attractive. Nevertheless, when a woman begins to exhibit ambiguous indications or displays signs of excessive apprehension, men inherently begin to ponder, "Uh oh...what might be amiss with her?"

It is worth bearing in mind that initial perceptions hold significant weight. On certain occasions, to our dismay, they persist indefinitely within an individual's consciousness.

Exhibiting self-restraint over anxious behavior and refraining from disclosing excessive personal information prematurely constitute a vital aspect of the courtship endeavor. Nevertheless, that particular facet of dating will be addressed at a subsequent juncture. For the time being, let us direct our attention towards the image you convey and its implications on your romantic endeavors. Now that you have gained a profound understanding of the significance of appearances in human communication, it is imperative to acquire the skills necessary to refine and restore your public image.

Chapter 4

Develop a healthy relationship.

Comprehending the nuances of an ideal relationship, particularly for individuals who have endured previous emotional harm, can be a complex endeavor. A single negative relationship can disrupt your equilibrium and erode your self-assurance, resulting in persistent self-doubt that may linger for an extended period. To access additional details, kindly refer to the resource titled "A Guide to Cultivating a Fulfilling and Harmonious Relationship."

Acknowledge that harmonious relationships inherently encompass certain measure of discord. Nevertheless, there has been a surge in the dissemination of promising research from esteemed institutions such as the Gottman Institute and other reputable organizations, thereby augmenting our society's comprehension of the behaviors conducive to fostering healthy relationships. Unexpectedly, the issue does not lie in the frequency of disputes within a relationship. It has been determined that all relationships possess unresolved matters, however contented couples are adept at tolerating these challenges. Alternatively: Through careful examination, it has come to light that each relationship bears unresolved concerns, notwithstanding that blissful couples are adept at navigating and accepting these difficulties.

A considerable proportion of high divorce rates can be attributed to the practice of repressing emotions and maintaining a facade of normalcy despite underlying issues. The probability of an unsuccessful marriage is also highly associated with feelings of contempt, engaging in eye-rolling behaviors, disregarding the other person's viewpoint, and displaying acts of disrespect. Males demonstrate heightened sensitivity to criticism, and robustly critical evaluations of males serve as a reliable predictor for divorce. Research findings indicate that cohabitation does not serve as a reliable predictor of future marital success; in fact, it may potentially exert a detrimental impact.

Experiencing an excess of emotions in an individual is a significant predictor of divorce. Give precedence to engaging in conversations with acquaintances, strategically organize your thoughts, and focus solely on articulating your emotions without engaging in any form of judgement. Expressing emotions such as sadness, feeling hurt, or anger would be more appropriate than stating 'You constantly...' In addition, it is worth noting that a significant contributing factor to divorce is the absence of love and affection, rather than just disagreements.

According to one article discussing Gottman's research, it states that individuals who established successful marriages were frequently affectionate and experienced a profound sense of love during the early stages of their union. In contrast to other couples, they exhibited lesser ambivalence, expressed negative emotions with lesser frequency, and held a more favorable perception of their partner. Significantly, these emotions remained constant over time.

It is crucial to refrain from adopting a condescending attitude towards your spouse, offering unsolicited advice, passing judgment, imposing curfews, or employing any other means to exert dominance over them. If we may discern, kindly withhold criticism regarding his methods, yet embrace his individuality and refrain from attempting to modify him. If you find it difficult to restrain your inclination, it would be advisable to allow him to seek companionship with a different woman who will appreciate him for his authentic self, rather than what you perceive as his possible future achievements, and who will genuinely understand his true worth. It is of utmost importance to seek out individuals who share your interests by attending suitable social settings. In order to establish a more lasting partnership, it is advisable to engage in a period of mutual acquaintance prior to entering into matrimony, preferably after a minimum of eight months from the initial encounter.

Each romantic relationship experiences both positive and negative moments, necessitating commitment, perseverance, and a willingness to adapt alongside one's partner. However, regardless of the duration of your dating experience or the novelty of your relationship, there exist various measures you can undertake to cultivate a thriving interpersonal connection. One can discover effective approaches to maintain a strong connection, cultivate a sense of fulfillment, and achieve long-lasting happiness, regardless of past relationship failures or challenges in revitalizing the intimacy within one's current relationship.

Dating College Mate
Engaging in a romantic relationship with a fellow college student can be an enjoyable and socially enriching experience. Furthermore, in addition, within the realm of higher education, one encounters a substantial amount of academic pressure to be concerned about. There is no necessity to

exacerbate your concerns by becoming excessively agitated about your planned social engagement. When encountering a peer in your academic cohort, do not hesitate to extend an invitation for social engagement. All of you have nothing to forfeit. The social aspect of college life is among its most thrilling attributes.

When engaging in romantic relationships with fellow classmates at the collegiate level, it is advantageous to leverage the shared interest inherent to your academic pursuits. Recognizing the fact that both of you are enrolled in the same class enhances the appropriateness and satisfaction of pursuing a romantic relationship.

In addition, it is conceivable that engaging in romantic partnerships during college may result in the formation of enduring relationships that encompass the institution of marriage. Despite the outcomes of studies indicating a mere two percent success rate in leading to a legitimate marital union. Nevertheless, refrain from unnecessarily conflating issues. Make an effort to allocate sufficient time for self-reflection, in order to ascertain the potential trajectory of the relationship. It is important to recognize that higher education is not an optimal period to engage in committed relationships; therefore, it is advised to refrain from overly pressuring yourself to partake in endeavors that may lead to future remorse.

The duration of this kind of relationship typically spans from a few months to two years, contingent upon the age of the individuals involved and the level of the relationship's quality. It is strongly recommended to refrain from prolonging a teenage relationship to prevent subsequent feelings of remorse in the future.

Female students enrolled in a collegiate institution are strongly recommended to adhere to the following guidelines:

It is strongly recommended that young women refrain from establishing close relationships with male individuals residing on their floor or within their hostel. It is advised to exercise caution and avoid rushing into any associations. However, it is important not to dismiss the prospect of acquainting oneself with male individuals who may approach one in due course. Occasionally, it is advisable to socialize with your peers from college rather than consistently engaging in nightly conversations with them. Please bear in mind that the primary purpose of your college experience is to pursue academic pursuits, rather than engaging in romantic relationships. In the event that you are inexperienced with dating or have recently ended a previous relationship, it would be judicious to ease into the dating scene gradually. Refrain from venturing out each evening.

Regarding romantic involvement with college peers, it is advisable to adopt an affirmative stance, approach it as an opportunity for leisure, while maintaining realistic expectations regarding establishing a long-term partnership. University seniors possess proficiency in casual relationships. It is crucial to exercise caution not to engage romantically with individuals who are already committed to someone else. If both of you reside at a significant distance from one another, it may be worth contemplating the cessation of your relationship due to the challenges imposed by long-distance circumstances. Refrain from engaging in romantic relationships within your immediate vicinity.

The dating experience in college is one that leaves a lasting impression for various reasons. In the period of attending college, numerous young individuals anticipate the opportunity to encounter a wide range of individuals and potentially cultivate intimate connections devoid of parental oversight, as well as the influence of figures of authority such as school or church officials. Nevertheless, it is important to take into account the following key factors before initiating a romantic relationship during one's college years.

1. Discipline: Restraint: Temperance:

Expressing the intention to exercise self-control in the context of dating during college may prove to be more challenging than initially anticipated. However, should you ultimately choose to pursue college dating, you will discover that cultivating self-discipline and a clear sense of personal identity will greatly benefit you in this realm. Frequently, individuals endeavor to present an altered version of themselves in order to appeal to others. While this approach may yield favorable results in certain instances, it typically proves challenging to sustain an artificial facade in order to maintain someone's interest.

Therefore, adopting an authentic demeanor is the optimal strategy when engaging in romantic relationships during one's time in higher education. This would enable individuals to become acquainted with your true persona. In addition, it is advisable to refrain from attempting to create a favorable impression on others, as it is arduous to relinquish one's true identity. Naturally, the practice of self-restraint necessitates a deep understanding of one's own self. Should you remain unfamiliar with yourself, it is advisable to allocate a considerable amount of time towards self-discovery prior to embarking on a romantic relationship with a fellow college student.

2. Ensure Safety during Playtime:

Engaging in relationships with fellow college students can provide an enjoyable experience. However, it is imperative to prioritize safety precautions when connecting with unfamiliar individuals. There have been numerous instances where young individuals have found themselves facing highly unforeseen circumstances during their romantic relationships. Certain occurrences, such as instances of date rape and stalking, are significantly more prevalent than commonly believed. As a result, it is imperative to adopt measures to ensure safety while engaging in dating activities. Should you experience any discomfort or concerns regarding the prospect of embarking on a solitary date with an individual, I would recommend considering the option of a group outing or selecting public venues that house a substantial number of individuals. This would provide a conducive environment for you until such time as you develop a sense of ease and security in the company of the aforementioned individual with whom you are romantically involved. Frequently, they sustain such malevolence by means of alcohol, and illicit substances often become catalysts for difficulties in romantic partnerships.

3. Acquire knowledge and derive enjoyment:

The college experience encompasses the pursuit of scholarly distinction, yet it does not preclude the possibility of engaging in leisurely activities and recreational pursuits. When you commence your journey in College, the distinctive milieu will acquaint you with a plethora of diverse individuals, thereby providing you the opportunity to engage in social interactions and romantic relationships with individuals whom you may not have previously considered pursuing.

While a portion of university contemporaries may desire to cultivate enduring romantic partnerships, it is noteworthy that the majority simply seek casual enjoyment, acquainting themselves with your preferences and progressing accordingly. This presents an exceptional chance to discern your preferences and priorities in a prospective partner.

4. Maintain a Proper Perspective on Sexual Matters:

Sexual activity should consistently be maintained as a secondary consideration, as numerous potentially advantageous relationships have been detrimentally affected by the premature inclusion of sexual encounters within the relationship. Rushing into a commitment without fully comprehending the individual can impose an immense emotional weight on the partnership, particularly when it has not yet developed the necessary maturity to withstand such a challenging burden. When sexual activity becomes a part of such a relationship, all aspects, including communication, undergo a significant transformation. Just as dating serves the purpose of cultivating a friendship, marriage serves the purpose of fostering deep emotional connection and intimacy.

Overall, the collegiate dating experience is characterized by its distinctiveness and inherent charm. It is imperative to bear in mind the necessity of engaging in safe practices, remaining true to one's authentic self, exercising self-discipline, and deriving enjoyment from the experience. Acquire the ability to maintain appropriate boundaries regarding sexual matters. The maximization of your dating experience during your time in college is entirely within your discretion.

Desirable Characteristics In Women Appreciated By Men

When discussing the attributes in women that are appreciated by men, I am referring to the deeper characteristics rather than the superficial aspects that often capture the attention of many individuals. Naturally, there will be individuals who possess a preference for specific hair hues, particular bust proportions, specific heights, and so forth. These are factors over which you have absolutely no agency, and it is imperative to recognize that males can often exhibit childlike behavior in a setting reminiscent of an ice cream parlor. If an individual demonstrates a preference for brunettes at present, it is likely that upon revisiting the topic in a few months, they will exhibit a strong inclination towards the redheaded individuals employed at their company. If you had made a alteration with the intention of conforming to his preferred attributes, you would find yourself regularly purchasing hair dyes at the store. When discussing qualities that are attractive to men, I am referring to personality traits that are malleable and open to modification if desired. These attributes possess the ability to contribute significantly to your personal growth over time and position you uniquely, rendering you appealing to the majority of the male population. Modifying both your hair color and breast size does not provide a suitable solution in this context.

Confidence is a desirable trait that is highly appreciated by a majority of men when seeking qualities in a woman. The essence of cultivating confidence lies in the art of projecting it, even when it may not naturally be present. This pertains to a personal characteristic that you possess, which, if modified, will result in significant advantages across various aspects of your life. Men are fond of observing a woman who exhibits a sense of confidence and authenticity in her own being. If you repeatedly seek validation from your partner regarding your appearance in a dress due to feeling self-conscious about your weight, it is likely that he will begin to doubt his choice in a partner and entertain the notion that your outward persona may not align with your true self. Despite any lack of confidence you may feel in your heels and dress, it is advisable to conceal this from him. There is an inherent allure to a young woman who maintains confidence in her appeal and sensuality, even during moments of subpar performance. When one maintains a perpetual aura of confidence in their appearance, it quickly captures the attention of gentlemen, arousing their curiosity to delve deeper.

Pursuing intellectual prowess is certainly a desirable trait that the majority of men seek in a female companion. Can you recall those individuals in our past high school days who utilized that specific characteristic to attract the attention of men? It is probable that those individuals have matured past that stage and subsequently sought a woman who possesses intelligence. Attempting to feign ignorance and dependence may elicit attraction from certain individuals in contemporary society; however, it is probable that they will exploit your vulnerability and ultimately pursue a woman who possesses intellectual autonomy. The issue arises when one assumes a facade of ignorance and dependence, with the intention of winning over the individual of interest. Once this person becomes weary of this charade, it becomes impossible to abruptly reveal that such behavior was a calculated strategy employed to capture their attention. Individuals will commence to question the veracity of other information you may have falsified and proceed to disengage promptly. Possessing intellectual capabilities does not necessitate the attainment of expertise in all matters; rather, it signifies the ability to independently make choices that will prove advantageous in the future. Men derive pleasure from relinquishing leadership responsibilities, and a woman possessing intellectual prowess exhibits greater allure than the most attractive supermodel of contemporary times.

Previously, I made reference to the allure of spontaneity in one's interaction with individuals of the male gender, elucidating on their inclination towards it. Upon discussing this topic with young women, their initial association is commonly linked to intimate interactions in a private setting. Exhibiting impulsiveness during intimate moments entails engaging in a spirited manner, as there exists an appropriate context and moment for such behavior. When I express that men prefer a woman who is spontaneous, I am referring to a woman who exhibits a willingness to adapt and make impromptu decisions whenever necessary. If one intends to dine out and discovers that the selected restaurant has ceased operation, an ideal companion suggests acquiring a hot dog and proceeding towards a cinematic experience on foot. Spontaneity is a quality that men appreciate due to its dual effects. Firstly, it alleviates the burden they face when being solely responsible for decision-making. Additionally, it eradicates the potential for a lack of engagement. Males may possess their established customs and routines, but a female individual who displays receptiveness to various experiences has the capacity to sustain the enthusiasm and passion over a significant span of time.

There is yet another attribute that I wish to discuss, and it is one that will prove advantageous in all your future interpersonal associations. Exhibiting sincerity is not a trait that one should adopt solely for the purpose of appeasing an individual of the male gender. By maintaining a sincere and open demeanor towards oneself and one's partner, one effectively eradicates the myriad of issues and conflicts that tend to plague most committed relationships on a daily basis. When one engages in dishonesty and conceals information, the dynamics of love transform into a situation of clinging to what one possesses, until the moment when the truth is uncovered. Demonstrating sincerity conveys to the individual that you are dependable with both their affection and confidential information. Men desire open communication in relationships, wherein they feel comfortable sharing all aspects of their lives with their partner, assured that no information will be concealed for the sole purpose of maintaining the relationship. If you can endeavor to cultivate a select few of these attributes, I assure you that any prospective individual towards whom you hold an affinity will encounter considerable difficulty in disengaging from your association. Let us proceed to the subsequent chapter to briefly engage in a discussion about characteristics in women that are disfavored by the male gender.

Utilizing The Principle Of Attraction

In accordance with the principles of the Law of Attraction, one has the ability to manifest desirable results through the deliberate cultivation of affirmative thoughts, grounded in the notion that similar energies naturally draw towards one another.

If you have been in search of your compatible life partner, understanding and following a set of uncomplicated guidelines will aid you in forging and drawing the lasting bond you desire.

When one possesses the knowledge and ability to harness and employ the boundless capabilities intrinsic to their being, there is no aspiration, action, or acquisition that remains beyond their reach.

The term "soulmate" refers to an individual who is ideally matched with another person in terms of temperament, or someone who closely resembles another person in attitudes or beliefs. It is worth mentioning that various portrayals of soulmates can be found in movies and folklore.

In fortunate instances, certain individuals possess the ability to forge a profound connection of the soul when they effortlessly and immediately resonate with one another. However, this does not imply that the process of identifying that particular individual was effortless.

Notwithstanding this fact, the procedure has the potential to be a pleasurable and advantageous experience.

Utilizing the Theory of the Law of Attraction to Uncover Your Ideal Life Partner

1. Articulate your authentic objectives with utmost clarity.

Each unsuccessful romantic partnership in the preceding times has bestowed upon you valuable insight into the qualities to seek in an exemplary life companion. The concern lies in the tendency of individuals to prioritize the negative aspects rather than the positive ones.

For example, when expressing your preference for a partner who does not prioritize their career over the relationship, you inadvertently draw attention to individuals who emphasize work over romance, thereby projecting this desire through your energy.

Fortunately, by being cognizant of your dislikes, you have the ability to ascertain your desires. Your aptitude for selecting unequivocal ideas to effectively convey your thoughts to the global audience is what empowers you to engage in meaningful creation. (As an example, "I desire a partner who prioritizes my needs and loves me unconditionally.")

Through the emotional response it elicits, one can discern whether an affirmation carries a positive or negative connotation. It would be deemed favorable if it contributes to your sense of well-being. It is deemed unfavorable if it evokes a negative emotional response. It is that simple.

Effortlessly shift your thought patterns by directing your attention towards the positive aspects whenever you detect the presence of negative thoughts. You will experience immediate feelings of improvement and establish a deep connection with affection.

2. Envision the desired affection and genuinely experience the sensation as though it is already present.

An effective strategy for individuals who are prepared to embrace love is to immerse oneself in contemplation of an idealized companion.

The cosmos views your visions of an ideal partner as guidelines for constructing your life accordingly. One has the ability to construct and enhance the desired connection in one's mind until it satisfies one's ideal criteria.

After conceptualizing that ideal image, continuously contemplate upon it until you inevitably manifest it in reality. Your imaginative faculty possesses an irresistibly influential capacity that could profoundly transform the course of your amorous endeavors.

3. Cultivate affection towards one's own identity.

We are capable of generating a force that alienates others when we subject ourselves to relentless and severe self-judgment. Engaging in self-criticism generates unfavorable vibes that could discourage potential partners.

Conversely, self-affection frequently possesses an allure that beckons prospective partners.

Compose a compilation of the foremost ten qualities that you hold in high regard about yourself, and prominently exhibit it in a location where you will encounter it on a daily basis. The specific items on the list hold no significance as long as they effectively cultivate a sense of self-affirmation.

As you redirect your attention towards your positive qualities, you will witness a gradual enhancement in your self-appreciation. Merely due to the profound sense of contentment that arises from being in the company of individuals possessing high self-esteem, others will consequently develop deep affection towards you.

4. Refuse to be envious.

It is justifiable to experience feelings of envy when witnessing another person derive pleasure from something that we desire but do not possess. Nonetheless, nurturing feelings of envy will hinder the arrival of love in your life. Jealousy, an exceptionally negative emotion, will impede you from attaining your aspirations.

Rather than experiencing jealousy, it is important to recognize that one's own goals are nearing realization when witnessing someone else's attainment.

Rather than experiencing jealousy, express joy for the love that you witness and express gratitude for the beautiful connections that you encounter. You are humbly beseeching the cosmos to bestow upon you a portion of its abundance through this manner.

What Are The Attributes That Women Find Appealing?

Naturally, in addition to discovering the ideal match, it is imperative to also cultivate personal perfection. A relationship ought to perpetually uphold a mutual exchange of efforts and contributions from both parties. It constitutes a reciprocal arrangement. You are entitled to achieving your desires and fulfilling your needs, and concurrently, it is imperative to ensure that your partner's wants and needs are similarly fulfilled. What steps must one take to attain perfection? While it is widely acknowledged that no individual can claim absolute perfection, it is important to consider that there are certain scenarios in which one can be perceived as flawless by another individual, irrespective of their inherent imperfections and fallibility. This outcome will occur upon achieving compatibility and suitability as their ideal partner. It is truly gratifying when one has the ability to bring joy to their life partner. It is imperative that you equally exert your efforts, just as she does.

Gaining insight into a woman's thoughts and deciphering her genuine preferences can be a formidable challenge. Certain individuals argue that the dynamics at play bear a striking resemblance to those experienced in the male realm, albeit with a reduced level of complexity. The majority of women are unlikely to express their attraction towards a man directly. It is probable that she would anticipate the gentleman to initiate an advance. Women believe that they ought to be the recipients of romantic gestures, and this sentiment is compounded by the belief that taking the initiative will hinder the likelihood of such gestures taking place. The majority of women tend to prefer men who exhibit dominance and are capable of leaving them awestruck.

For certain women, embodying qualities of accountability and dependability holds utmost significance. It entails not only establishing a permanent residence, but also assuming accountability for their life choices. They possess a clear understanding of their priorities and exhibit maturity by refraining from engaging in frivolous behavior while in pursuit of their life partners. Acquiring a woman's affection is, in fact, a task that can be accomplished with relative ease. Exhibit unwavering loyalty and remain steadfastly loyal. While it is not the sole determinant, it significantly contributes to the longevity of a relationship. Certainly, no one desires to associate themselves with an individual who engages in deceitful behavior. A relationship rooted in infidelity is certainly destined for a short lifespan. Assume accountability for your actions and choices.

It is often stated that initial impressions carry enduring significance, and there are women who desire their male partners to exhibit a dominant nature. One cannot assert dominance when exhibiting a slouchy demeanor, laziness, and a reluctance to present oneself in an orderly manner. You are not going to rectify yourself solely for the purpose of impressing women. Additionally, it will foster a sense of self-esteem and gratification. As one cultivates a sense of inner well-being, their mindset becomes optimistic, consequently attracting a series of favorable circumstances. When one experiences inner happiness, it becomes apparent externally, thereby captivating the interest of numerous women drawn to your positive energy. You need not adhere to the standards set by Calvin Klein models in order to be perceived positively by women. However, it would certainly be advantageous if you do not appear disheveled or unkempt. One's demeanor and comportment are the determining factors.

Women similarly appreciate the company of men who possess a capacity for comprehending them. Please make an effort to comprehend their perspective. It can be challenging to gain a comprehensive understanding of women. It is not inherent in the nature of individuals of the male gender to possess sensitivity; however, it is imperative that earnest efforts be made to exhibit receptiveness and empathy towards the desires and emotions of individuals of the female gender. If they perceive an indifference towards their emotions emanating from you, their interest in you will assuredly wane. It is important to acknowledge that women tend to exhibit emotional characteristics inherently. Grant them adequate personal space when it is required. It is important to also consider the distressing experience they endure on a monthly basis. You should refrain from passing judgment on that particular experience, as you will never truly comprehend its associated emotions. It entails navigating the intricate dynamics of a woman's mind and body, demonstrating sensitivity and providing optimal support to her during this tumultuous journey.

A women's possession of a humorous disposition is equally pivotal. They are prone to being attracted to individuals who have the ability to consistently evoke laughter. Occasionally, the emphasis on one's appearance takes a backseat. Despite lacking physical attractiveness, numerous women would be inclined to pursue a relationship with a man if he possesses a remarkable sense of humor. He consistently keeps things engaging, and has the ability to infuse even the most mundane situations with enjoyment and thrill. Many women seek partners who fit this description. It is a remarkable advantage when a gentleman discovers a woman who possesses a remarkable sense of humor.

Females also appreciate it when males maintain a consistent attitude throughout the entire duration. Certain individuals alter their behavior towards their female partners upon reaching a particular stage in the relationship. This will engender feelings of insignificance and underappreciation among women. Ensure to consistently demonstrate attentiveness and appreciation towards your significant other, as reciprocation is highly probable should you fulfill this obligation. If any issues arise, it is advisable to convene a discussion in order to address them. One should not immediately purchase a new residence solely in response to a defective ceiling in their current dwelling. You fix the ceiling. This is the prescribed manner in which a relationship ought to function. Every woman possesses an inherent sense of regal grace. They desire to be pursued and courted with charm and grace. It is not always the case, but a gentleman should understand that even after winning a woman's affection, the process of courtship should persist.

These qualities represent the foundational attributes that women seek in men. Additional attributes such as well-groomed hair, captivating eyes, and a fit physique are merely inconsequential factors. The physical appearance of a man is subject to the preferences of the woman. Certain women are attracted to men with well-defined musculature, others are attracted to slender physiques, and still others are drawn to more ample body types. The preferences may vary, but every woman desires a partner who possesses the ability to comprehend and provide the necessary support. Possess these traits and you will undoubtedly become an appealing prospect for them; however, it is crucial to refrain from altering your authentic identity solely to elicit attraction from women. Certain individuals assume different personas in order to deceive women. You are destined to experience discontentment, while simultaneously engaging in a mutual falsehood. Remain steadfast and remain true to your authentic self. Each individual possesses inherent uniqueness, and it is certain that there exists someone who will undoubtedly be captivated by your true self.

He Is Not Seeking A Companion For Play; Rather, He Seeks A Partner To Assist Him.

Males consistently exhibit a desire to engage in recreational activities, whereas adult males consistently exhibit a desire to engage in productive tasks. Male individuals actively search for companions to engage in recreational activities, whereas adult males actively search for support and aid.

Are you able to comprehend the point I am trying to convey?

The individual whom God has designated for you does not engage in frivolous behavior or feign immaturity. He possesses a strong sense of determination and clear direction regarding his life goals and aspirations, as well as his objectives within his personal relationships. Deceptive behaviors, reluctance to make a commitment, discourtesy, and various other disagreeable conduct do not serve as signs of a man genuinely dedicated to being in a relationship with you. The gentleman who is suitable for you does not seek to rely on you or exploit your assistance.

He yearns for a partnership with you, to construct alongside you, to embrace you, and to dedicate resources towards your growth. It is imperative for you to acknowledge the trend exhibited by individuals who have a mere desire to engage in recreational activities. A considerable number of individuals, including your acquaintances and relatives, frequently succumb to these pitfalls. The indications of potential danger are evident. One can either observe these traits and attributes or completely overlook them, resulting in a failure to discern between a man's sincere intentions and his propensity for engaging in deceptive behavior.

The issue of men who display uncertainty regarding their desires poses a common predicament for women. He is uncertain about his readiness for a romantic commitment or the direction in which he wishes to steer it. Let us temporarily embrace a more adaptable approach. We should avoid excessive contemplation or placing excessive burden on ourselves...

That is a frequently used expression among males, and if it has been communicated to you, it is highly probable that he is engaging in manipulative behavior. He is providing you with misleading information, and to be frank, he does not seem particularly concerned. He possesses clear awareness of his desires, yet refrains from disclosing them due to his apprehension regarding their unattainability.

As an illustration, consider the scenario whereby you encounter an individual who overtly seeks sexual encounters but purports to desire casual enjoyment. He desires a tranquil environment in which he can unwind, indulge in leisure activities, encounter contentment amongst all individuals, absence of complaints, and unrestricted freedom to engage in any desired actions.

Nevertheless, he lacks the capacity to convey this information to you. Regardless of the number of women who suggest that if a man is seeking solely physical intimacy, he should be forthright about his intentions in order to potentially attain it, there is an extremely slim likelihood, approximately one percent, of this scenario materializing. It must be noted, however, that this estimation is exaggerated, and the actual probability of success lies at a meager 0.01 percent in the overwhelming majority of such instances.

It will be deactivated by you. Why? Because the vast majority of women are not pursuing a scenario of that nature. When you consider it, it is highly probable that it is because you have become fatigued with relationships or you are in pursuit of something expedient and uncomplicated due to not having completely recuperated from past letdowns. Despite its occasional inconvenience, your inclination towards seeking companionship through less risky means stems from a fear of vulnerability and reluctance to expose yourself to potential harm.

You find yourself in a predicament with no clear solution.

You hinder a genuine, comprehensive association due to your apprehension that it will engender grief and disillusionment. Consequently, you appreciate the concepts of "enjoyment," "simplicity," and "efficiency." Even if you consider this connection to be unfavourable, the consequences are modified when a man openly expresses his authentic objectives. It becomes more difficult to accept when he expresses to you, 'I perceive you solely as a companion for casual interaction.'

You are at ease with this notion because it grants you an illusionary sense of authority when verbalized- the act of expressing that you perceive him merely as a companion, despite his feelings for you and desire for a deeper connection. Nevertheless, his directness does not sit well with you. In spite of assertions made by certain women, it is generally recognized by the majority of men that being straightforward may not necessarily yield favorable outcomes in situations of casual sexual encounters. So, what is the alternative? They deceive you.

I unequivocally disapprove of the false statement and offer no validation or justification for it. Nevertheless, I am confident that numerous individuals have attempted the straightforward approach but encountered setbacks. Males are aware that adopting an indirect approach and suggesting a flexible outlook enhances the likelihood of achieving their desires. Hence, they will provide you with whatever is necessary to sustain the situation and prolong its progression.

Be a steadfast companion to a man whenever he desires to adopt a passive approach. Avoid engaging in a romantic relationship with a man who displays uncertainty regarding his desires or professes ignorance. Once he attains comprehension, he may make another attempt, and thereafter, both of you can engage in a discussion regarding the appropriate course of action. Engaging in such circumstances can lead to calamitous outcomes. By acknowledging his lack of lucidity and purpose, he enables himself to evade accountability and extend the duration of the crisis. It is not beyond the realm of possibility that circumstances may change, however, the probability of such a shift occurring is extremely remote. When making decisions, it is prudent to carefully evaluate what is most advantageous and feasible in light of your own well-being. According to divine will, it is not deemed suitable to engage in a romantic relationship with an individual who lacks the willingness to fully commit to you.

Why do you remain in a committed relationship with a gentleman who fails to acknowledge your status as his spouse and demonstrates no intention of formalizing your union?

What would be the reasoning behind your desire to consider such a scenario?

It is unadvisable to engage with an individual who lacks clarity regarding their desires.

Cease the act of anticipating his readiness.

A prevalent belief among some is that it is necessary to wait until he indicates his readiness, and that one should be prepared when he eventually decides he is prepared for a committed relationship. I have engaged in conversations with numerous women who hold this perspective, and their stance is as follows: Although he has not yet reached the desired level of commitment, I am choosing to remain a part of his life. I will demonstrate to him my qualities as a respectable individual, ensuring that when he reaches a stage of personal growth and maturity suitable for commitment, he selects me as the suitable partner for such a significant undertaking.

That\\\'s a terrible strategy.

Primarily, you are not considered a runner-up. Just because a man is fatigued from pursuing various endeavors and is willing to commit to the woman who has supported him, does not necessarily indicate that he is in love with her. It does not signify his desire to engage in your company, gratify your needs, or invest his attention and effort in you. Rest assured that I am not fabricating this assertion as I affirm that he selected you as the only remaining option. I have been informed by individuals that their marital partners chose them as a result of limited alternatives.

In the barbershop, a gentleman conveyed to me that he selected his spouse, the woman with whom he entered into matrimony, solely due to her being the sole available option. She was the individual who remained by his presence. What\\\'s more, guess what? He does not possess genuine affection for her. It is unsurprising, nonetheless, that they are encountering difficulties. It is scarcely astonishing that he is contemplating departure. It is not desirable for him to choose you solely due to your presence when he regained consciousness.

Additionally, it is improbable that he will spontaneously conclude at some point that he desires it. It is a gradual process of transformation, a matter he has contemplated and may continue to contemplate even in your presence. However, as I have mentioned earlier, his repeated assertion of indecisiveness or lack of readiness is merely a facade to conceal my belief that I do not perceive YOU as the suitable candidate. The intention behind this message is not to cause any harm or distress, but rather to convey the understanding that your presence may not be suitable in that particular setting. Frankly speaking, there is no issue with his lack of perception of you as "the one" since he is clearly not the suitable individual for you.

To reach a definitive conclusion that he is not the suitable partner for you and it is more beneficial for you to disengage, it is imperative to engage in introspection, engage in prayer, carefully evaluate any warning signs, and address all challenges.

Avoid the error of anticipating his readiness.

Oftentimes, it is the woman who patiently awaits who eventually awakens to find him departing alongside someone else. He proceeds with his life and enters into matrimony with another individual. He explicitly communicates his lack of readiness for marriage and a committed partnership. However, after the passage of three months, a sudden change occurs.

He\\\'s Betrothed.

Evidently, the matter of being prepared was not a concern; rather, it was merely a matter of him not choosing you. Once more, I comprehend that this information may cause discomfort for certain individuals.

I comprehend, nevertheless I am compelled to articulate the veracity. It can be likened to consuming a bitter-tasting medication that is ultimately advantageous for one's well-being. You will experience a significant improvement in your well-being upon assimilating, acknowledging, and progressing from the situation. Do not succumb to the idea of deferring until he is prepared.

Exercise caution when interpreting contradictory messages.

The next factor that should be taken into account pertains to the matter of conflicting messages. Many males cause confusion for you, which is quite comprehensible. They make the following statement, "I have no desire for a romantic partner, but I desire to behave in a manner consistent with being in a relationship." They express sentiments such as, "I do not wish for a committed partnership, yet I want to influence and determine the people with whom you interact and engage," which presents some confusion.

They desire to engage in intimate and enjoyable activities, yet when inquired about the trajectory of the relationship, he responds with an admonishment to remain composed, asserting that one is progressing too hastily. One is compelled to question the nature and purpose of his actions.

Indeed, it is quite baffling, but allow me to share something with you.

Online Dating For Women

The female demographic accounts for 48% of the overall population of individuals utilizing dating platforms. Despite a slight numerical disadvantage compared to men, women often constitute the prevailing demographic on numerous dating websites. Ladies exhibit a great inclination towards engaging in conversation, as they possess an exceptional capacity for generating an abundance of topics for discussion. This disparity in response arises from the fact that certain individuals may feel inclined to avoid women who display excessive confidence and strength, while others embrace the prospect of being engaged in stimulating interactions.

Stay Away from Photoshop

Despite the preeminence of men's visual tendencies, they actively seek out women of substance. Approximately 42% of male users on online dating platforms exhibit a preference for individuals categorized as the "modern career-oriented woman." They seek a candidate who possesses not only aesthetic appeal, but also demonstrates a commendable degree of self-sufficiency, strength, and assurance. These characteristics have a magnetic effect on men as, in current times, establishing a family necessitates significant dedication and collaborative effort.

Please refrain from excessively altering your facial features or physique. Please refrain from entertaining the thought of engaging in such activities. Have faith in your innate beauty and others will discern the aura of self-assurance emanating from your photographic representation. Is it not delightful to capture someone's attention solely through the allure of your innate beauty? If your objective is to pursue true love, approach it authentically. Do not rely on superficiality, instead, assert yourself with uniqueness.

Kindly ensure that you have a few aesthetically pleasing photographs of yourself available for submission, preferably including a full-body image. Abandon the use of Photoshop, for your innate excellence is already remarkable. Demonstrate to others your ability to engage in meaningful interaction, while showcasing how your spontaneous nature adds to your charisma. Gentlemen prefer the company of women who engage in meaningful discussions regarding substantial topics, rather than merely focusing on cosmetics or other superficial subjects.

Generally, Coyness Works

One may entertain the notion that in the present era, coyness is no longer imperative due to the advancement into the 21st century. However, it is quite the contrary as men derive satisfaction from exerting effort to obtain what they desire. Significant accomplishments should not be easily attained, and gentlemen appreciate the worth of a woman who does not readily avail herself to a man.

Indeed, it is true that several individuals of the male gender may necessitate a clear indication that permits them to actively pursue your acquaintance. Nonetheless, it is crucial to acknowledge that the realm of online dating functions under a distinct set of principles and dynamics. It is not permissible to initiate communication with individuals encountered online, however, one may appropriately respond when efforts are made to attract one's attention. Avoid displaying overt and immediate interest towards an individual of the male gender. This can frequently result in disinterest as the pursuit has concluded.

Instead, entice his interest by strategically revealing certain aspects of yourself that will leave him wanting to know more. Exercise caution in displaying excessive assertiveness, as your keen interest in him may inadvertently contribute to the inflation of his ego. The male ego, though delicate, can be leveraged to exploit the natural attraction that women have towards it. If he were to, indeed, decide to distance himself despite your earnest endeavors to express your attraction, you may find yourself growing increasingly disheartened.

Don't Break the Dam

A significant influx of personal information could potentially have adverse outcomes as individuals of the male gender often exhibit a comparatively slower pace in terms of fostering deeper connections. Despite the extended duration of your conversations with him, it is still prudent to exercise restraint when disclosing personal information about yourself. Do exercise caution in ensuring that he is not exposed to an excessive amount of information that may lead to feelings of overwhelm. Although it is apparent that you desire him to perceive your interest, unveiling your emotions in an unrestricted manner will only inundate him.

Online dating may present itself as a rapid and dynamic method of seeking romantic connections, however, it should not be confused with the concept of speed dating. It constitutes yet another mechanism for the establishment of bonds. It remains imperative to afford your potential future partner sufficient room for contemplation concerning the conversations and information shared, pertaining to each other. A considerable number of women display interest in acquiring further knowledge about the men in their lives, often posing inquiries concerning personal matters. Conversely, men tend to exhibit dissimilar behavior in this regard. Ensure that your online dating experience flows seamlessly like a continuous stream of water. It instills tranquility within the innermost being and infuses vitality into the course of one's journey.

Look Beyond the Photo

Women also demonstrate a considerable emphasis on visual attributes when seeking a lifelong partner. Why? From a biological standpoint, it is often observed that women have a preference for men who demonstrate advantageous genetic traits through symmetrical physical characteristics. Certain women have a propensity for specific eye hues, as they harbor a "desire" to unite in matrimony with individuals possessing those particular eye colors. Nevertheless, the gentleman's capacity to provide support in the event of a potential union holds greater significance than his physical traits.

In the present context, the term 'support' encompasses both fiscal and emotional dimensions. Women have a fundamental requirement for affection, and it is not surprising that certain women may still desire a partner who diligently caters to their necessities. I assume that you would not prefer to be the sole individual engaged in the task, correct? If your partner does not exert the necessary effort, your relationship will swiftly deteriorate.

Similarly, it is imperative that your partner possesses a disposition of compassion and sensitivity. Princes do not solely possess material wealth or financial stability. They should possess an ample amount of love and compassion to impart. The succeeding section will provide further details on this matter.

The concept of being wealthy or affluent does not necessarily equate to garnering respect and love.

Certain relationships experience dissolution due to instances of both physical and verbal abuse. Primarily, if not exclusively, it is women who bear the brunt of derogatory language and harmful actions. It proves to be a rather arduous task to ascertain an individual's propensity for violence and instability. Consequently, the implementation of research is imperative in order to address this matter effectively.

Do not wholly depend on the contents of a gentleman's profile on the dating website. Instead, endeavor to gather additional information regarding his background through an examination of his various online platforms. Google serves as an invaluable repository containing a plethora of pertinent information. You may also verify the gentleman's potential involvement in any criminal activities by reviewing the news. While this may appear somewhat extreme, numerous women express remorse for not prioritizing thorough investigation during their pursuit of an ideal partner on online dating platforms.

Love cannot be measured by monetary value. Merely displaying an attractive automobile on his profile does not guarantee that he will demonstrate proper treatment towards you. Indeed, it would be prudent to afford him an opportunity for demonstrating his commendable traits, yet exercising caution is paramount when fostering an emotional connection with an individual through online means.

Exhibiting reverence and compassion can be instrumental in persevering through financial hardship, thus underscoring the paramount importance of these attributes in one's search for optimal qualities. Allow wealth to serve as an additional advantage, rather than a primary determinant, when evaluating a man's suitability as a partner or spouse. One can ascertain the individual's character and personality by considering the opinions and remarks of others regarding him. The majority of dating websites feature a designated "comments" section within the user profiles.

The Fundamental Truth Underlying The Principle Of The Law Of Attraction

Now that you possess a comprehensive understanding of the constituents that constitute the law of attraction, it is imperative that I address an additional aspect prior to delving into the procedure by which you can effectively employ the law of attraction. The law of attraction is underpinned by a crucial reality, and unless you possess a clear understanding of this fundamental truth, it is unlikely to yield favorable outcomes for you.

Many individuals hold the belief that the law of attraction is predominantly influenced by external factors. Now, you may be skeptically pondering and vocalizing your doubts regarding the plausibility of this assertion. Ultimately, the principle of the law of attraction centers upon the transformation of one's thought processes. By their very nature, thoughts are internal. Nevertheless, it remains true that the prevailing perception of the law of attraction frequently revolves around its external implications. Allow us to consider an alternate perspective: individuals frequently perceive the law of attraction in a comparable manner to how individuals seeking to lose weight perceive weight-loss products.

In general, individuals seeking to reduce their weight often opt to purchase dietary supplements, enroll in a weight management program, or engage in physical activity at a fitness center. They approach the procedure by seeking external entities, such as software, merchandise, or assistance, which is then employed to yield a desired outcome. This exemplifies an external perspective. Essentially, you are seeking external resources to serve as a means to achieve your goal. Any potential internal modifications are merely transitory in nature, as the primary emphasis remains on the external product, which serves as a means to achieve a particular objective.

It is evident from the substantial revenue generated by the global weight-loss industry, amounting to billions of dollars, that this industry remains resilient and displays no indications of waning. The externalist philosophy proves to be ineffective. If you desire the law of attraction to genuinely operate in your favor, refraining from perceiving it as a mere instrument is imperative. On the contrary, it is entirely intrinsic.

The law of attraction instills a sense of fear in numerous individuals. They exhibit a lack of willingness to undergo alterations. They possess an aversion towards undergoing the frequently distressing and arduous procedure of sincerely confronting their inner selves, as my previous chapters have clearly emphasized that the law of attraction mandates a significant level of honesty. In essence, the crux of the matter is that the law of attraction revolves entirely around personal transformation.

You embody the process.

I have delineated the law of attraction as a procedure. It commences with the inception of one's thoughts, subsequently encompassing multiple elements, culminating in the manifestation of a precise outcome. It is quite effortless to become trapped at either end of this procedure. It is fairly simple for individuals to perceive and comprehend the perceptual aspect. They think that, "OK. It pertains to the alteration of my thought processes. "The crux of the matter lies in the transformation of my internal constructs." Likewise, it comes effortlessly for them to observe the outcomes. It should be readily apparent.

We each harbor aspirations for desired outcomes. Each of us possesses desired outcomes. It is the proceedings that occur in the midst of the situation that truly perplex individuals. For certain individuals, this can be quite daunting as it involves significant exertion. Ultimately, when one effectively incorporates the principles of the law of attraction into their daily life, a transformative process occurs, resulting in a notable change in one's personal identity. Upon deep contemplation, it becomes abundantly clear that this notion is entirely logical, as one's core identity and thought processes remain unchanged. Consequently, it is hardly astonishing that the outcomes one experiences correspond to their current actions.

If you encounter challenges in your pursuit of attracting an appropriate individual, or if you find it difficult to attract a desirable individual presently, and you persist in employing the same strategies, it should come as no surprise that you fail to attract the desired individual. This scenario bears resemblance to the renowned statement attributed to Albert Einstein, wherein he remarked, "The definition of insanity is performing identical actions repeatedly while anticipating disparate outcomes."

The outcomes you achieve are a direct result of the actions you take. The outcomes that you achieve are a direct reflection of your thought processes and actions. The concept of the law of attraction revolves around transforming one's identity. It employs this methodology incorporating a diverse array of elements in order to foster novel thinking, ultimately yielding varied outcomes. Please find below an analysis of the functioning of the law of attraction, including the corresponding terminology used in this context.

Commence with a concept

The construction of reality occurs at the cognitive level. For instance, in the scenario where you are presently engaged in your professional occupation and upon receiving your wages, you ascertain that the sum is insufficient, it can be observed that this situation originated from a thought process. The notion is that, "This is the sole occupation within my capabilities." "This is the suitable employment opportunity for me." The precise notion, regardless of its nature, adheres to similar sentiments. It ultimately culminates in your present career position, where you perceive an inadequate level of compensation. The entire process commences with a cognitive process and is subsequently solidified through additional cognitive processes.

As per the principle of the law of attraction, this is the "resonance" we transmit to the world. Should you choose not to alter the existing vibrational state, do not anticipate a modification in the ultimate outcome. Do not anticipate an increase in the figures presented on your pay cheque. It is highly unlikely for that to occur.

Focus

The subsequent phase in the progression of self-development entails directing your attention towards your cognitive faculties. The greater the level of effort exerted, the increased probability of acting upon that concept. For instance, should someone have caused harm in the past and your thoughts persistently dwell on the pain inflicted upon you, leaving you feeling foolish, your subsequent course of action would likely be one characterized by apprehension towards potential future hurts. This holds you back. Why? Since you have elected to concentrate on that particular recollection in such a manner.

If one engages in thorough self-reflection and critically deconstructs that particular memory, delving deep into the objective truths underlying it, one would likely discern the existence of a potential alternative interpretation for that memory. This alternative interpretation could potentially yield conclusions that are less incapacitating. One tends to minimize self-criticism and enhance self-esteem and self-value. The crux of the matter centers on concentration. We possess an immense level of concentration. Regrettably, we frequently allow our attention to hinder us rather than benefit us. Is it not the opportune moment to harness our capacity to concentrate in order to propel our aspirations forward, rather than allowing it to impede our progress?

Chapter 4: Good Impressions

Love permeates the atmosphere, yet the lingering inquiry plaguing those who are unattached is its validity.

One might encounter love in various unexpected settings; perhaps while leisurely strolling through a quaint café amidst a delightful sunlit afternoon, or even during a serene lakeside excursion on a balmy day. It would be advisable for you to conduct a thorough search for it. Engage in the exploration of potential possibilities, and in due course, an exceptional opportunity will manifest itself.

In light of such a delectable situation, how ought one proceed?

When one encounters another person (especially an individual of great importance), it is of paramount importance to establish a favorable impression, particularly in the context of business encounters. By adopting this approach, you can prevent others from developing a diminished perception of your character. Conversely, if you convey an attitude of self-neglect, it is likely to diminish their regard for you. You have the freedom to choose your attire, however, allow me to offer some suggestions to ensure that you create a favorable impression on your romantic partner.

One effective strategy for creating a positive impression is to attire oneself in a sophisticated manner. Your attire and overall demeanor serve as reflections of your identity. Please ensure that your attire is tastefully sophisticated, avoiding excessive opulence that may be perceived as intimidating. Attire yourself in a manner that prioritizes both comfort and presentability, avoiding extravagance that would lead to an untidy appearance. Please ensure that you select attire that is suitable for the occasion, in order to avoid any negative impressions that others may form about you. Dress in a manner that epitomizes a commendable representation of yourself. It is recommended that, on a first date, one adopts an attire characterized by elegance, refinement, and a hint of personal style. By adopting this approach, you will effectively distinguish yourself from others while simultaneously avoiding the potential risk of being subject to derision.

The next method to create a positive impression involves your personal hygiene and appearance, encompassing both your attire and conduct. For gentlemen, ensure that your facial hair is well-groomed, either by maintaining a neatly trimmed beard or by being cleanly shaven. In regard to women, it is advisable not to excessively emphasize your makeup. Rather, consider applying it in a manner that complements and accentuates your natural beauty. When you find yourself on a romantic outing with someone, it is crucial to exhibit appropriate decorum, as it serves as a demonstration of your commitment to showing respect and admiration for the other person, even through seemingly insignificant gestures.

Another crucial factor in creating a favorable impression would be the manner in which you articulate your words. Given your desire to create a favorable impression, it is essential that you articulate your thoughts with clarity and certainty. Being a person of soft-spoken nature, it can sometimes pose a challenge for others to hear me unless they are accustomed to my manner of speaking. Typically, when encountering unfamiliar individuals, I tend to project my voice slightly louder than I do when conversing with my acquaintances. Such a practice increases the likelihood of one's spoken words being retained in the memory of others. If you are in the midst of a social encounter with an individual, it is recommended that you refrain from creating an overly subdued and serious atmosphere. Kindly share your finest jokes or most amusing anecdotes. Such captivating narratives will undoubtedly engage others and establish a perception of your broad range of interests and experiences.

Finally, it is essential that your body language serves to convey the unspoken messages that are not articulated by your verbal communication. A more formal way to express the same idea could be: "The concept of a closed impression refers to the physical posture of crossing one's arms or legs while placing an object as a barrier between oneself and the individual with whom one is conversing." A receptive or attentive demeanor would entail inclining slightly forward and displaying heightened involvement in the discussion. If you were to cross your legs, they wouldn't be tightly intertwined but rather resemble the numeral four. Numerous indicators exist that can determine whether someone is intriguing or uninteresting, and the reverse is also true.

In summary, it is advisable to conscientiously observe one's environment and companion, adjust one's approach based on the specific circumstances, and endeavor to establish a harmonious connection by aligning personalities in a distinct manner, thereby creating a sense of comfort and relaxation in their presence. This will facilitate smoother interactions, leading to a significantly enjoyable experience for both individuals involved. It is essential to bear in mind that achieving a flawless impression entails preserving the authenticity of your undead zombie self, rather than transforming into an artificial Barbie/Ken doll. The key lies in presenting the best version of your "cute and undead zombie" persona. This guidance holds utmost significance as your ultimate goal should be for your significant other to develop genuine affection for the true essence of your being, rather than merely falling for a superficial façade.

RECONNECTING BACK TO SELF

1. DETERMINE YOUR GOAL

You are under no obligation to exhibit, distribute, contribute, or generate below your full potential. Gaining awareness of your capabilities and uncovering your genuine sources of motivation can be achieved through the process of reestablishing a connection with oneself. The greater comprehension you possess in this matter, the more aptly you will be equipped to extend your support to others and enact meaningful change in the world surrounding you. It is time to explore and uncover the genuine sources of your motivation. What is the source of your utmost happiness? Your life\\\'s work.

At what point in time did you experience the greatest happiness? What activities do I engage in when I find myself in a state of heightened vulnerability?

What strategies can be employed to establish a sense of self-awareness in moments of solitude? That is your gift. Your very soul. The fundamental principle to reestablishing a connection with one's true self.

Discovering your true vocation can prove to be a challenging endeavor. Humans find themselves ensnared in disempowering patterns that perpetuate an unceasing cycle of nonachievement. We hold predetermined beliefs about our own capabilities and limitations in the realm of personal achievements. We adhere to an established happiness framework that has not been of our own making, permitting societal or familial obligations to impose demands upon us. We relentlessly pursue wealth, authority, and prestige, often devoid of any meaningful purpose or broader context, and it is through this lack of connection that we inevitably experience defeat.

2. Comprehend and fulfill your requirements.

Your purpose is intricately connected to the Six Human Needs, namely, the desire for assurance, significance, diversity, affection/association, personal development, and the act of making a positive impact. Although it is true that all individuals possess these six needs, each person exhibits a prevailing one.

The driving force behind our actions and decisions, and upon fulfillment, brings about a sense of happiness.

If one desires to effectuate a meaningful impact in the global sphere, it is highly likely that their inherent talent lies in the realm of altruistic endeavors such as engaging in volunteer work or actively pursuing acts of benevolence. If an individual seeks purpose or affiliation in their life, it is probable that their endeavors will revolve around familial and social relationships. Once you have discerned your fundamental human requirement, you may commence the process of acquiring the knowledge and skills to restore your connection with oneself.

Do not allow restrictive beliefs to persuade you that you are undeserving of having your basic needs fulfilled. Cease prioritizing the needs of others at all times without first attending to your own well-being. Once you have determined your requirements, fulfill them accordingly. Allocate some time for personal self-care and reflection. Request what you require from others. Maximizing your potential empowers you to contribute more effectively from a position of resilience and fortitude.

3. DISCOVER YOUR VOICE

Our voices are typically perceived in relation to their functionality, serving as a means of communication, self-expression, and providing amusement.

As per Edwin Coppard, a widely recognized global voice coach who has previously spoken at Life Wealth Mastery, our vocal expressions serve as a conduit to genuine inner self-affiliation.

Our vocal expressions were characterized by their innate purity and untainted nature during our youthful years. They emitted a high volume and forceful presence, and during our conversations, there was an absence of any form of restraint or censorship. As we matured and developed a deeper awareness of our environment, as well as our identity within it, we gradually repressed our innate voice in favor of adopting a socialized mindset.

The prevalence of a socialized mindset prevents us from fully attaining the profound vitality and potency inherent in the sounds of nature.
During our conversation, we assumed the role of societal ideals and personas,

ceasing to represent our individual selves.

We can move aside, enabling our inherent wisdom to guide us, and reconnect with the exquisite essence of the "untamed vocal expression" by means of the musical force. By utilizing the power of your vocal expression, you can effectively establish a connection with your inner child, simultaneously acquiring the skills necessary for self-communication Commence vocalizing in sync with your preferred musical composition. Compose your own unique composition. Acquire the proficiency of playing a musical instrument. Music possesses the capacity to awaken the depths of one's inner being.

4.RECONNECT PHYSICALLY WITH YOURSELF

Dance represents a formidable mode of self-expression. However, it is noteworthy that it has the potential to aid individuals in determining methods by which they can reestablish a connection with their own selves. That encapsulates the fundamental nature of the 5 Rhythms.

Gabrielle Roth was the originator and founder of the 5 Rhythms movement, which emerged in the latter part of the 1970s. It fundamentally encompasses the practice of meditative movement and dance. Roth posited that inducing bodily activity can unburden the heart, liberate the mind, and enable students to establish a profound connection with the genuine core of their being. This connection serves as the wellspring of inspiration, harboring boundless creativity and untapped potential. This theory is grounded in the belief that active movement has the capacity to foster self-fulfillment.

The five aforementioned rhythms, namely flowing, staccato, chaos, lyrical, and stillness, pertain to experiential patterns that delineate mental and emotional terrains, as opposed to sonic rhythms such as those produced by drums or beats. To put it differently, they can be equated with states of existence. The student assigns distinct interpretations to each rhythm, with the aim of facilitating mindful, unpredictable, and imaginative movement. Sequential application of these rhythms culminates in a "wave" that fosters a profound comprehension of one's innate authenticity, while simultaneously reestablishing a mind-body connection for grounding purposes.

5. BEGIN A JOURNAL

The art of writing, akin to music, vocals, cadence, and movement, can facilitate a profound connection with one's inner self. By documenting the impact of events and experiences on your psyche, you can enhance your capacity to recognize and embrace your emotions. Jotting down your emotions pertaining to present circumstances or occurrences experienced throughout the day can assist in the clarification of your thoughts. Transcribing your thoughts can contribute to their consolidation.

"My purpose in writing is to unearth the depths of my own knowledge," expressed esteemed American author Flannery O'Connor. It has the potential to validate your preexisting self-awareness.

Engaging in the practice of journaling yields benefits that transcend the mere act of self-reflection. It has the potential to facilitate relaxation, enhance cognitive retention, and foster a shift in one's perspective. It has the potential to aid you in directing your attention towards the positive aspects. It has the potential to facilitate the accomplishment of your objectives.

Acquiring confidence and obtaining a pen and journal are all it takes - however, the cultivation of a novel practice necessitates commitment. Allocate a portion of your daily schedule to engage in the practice of writing, even if it's only a brief duration of five minutes. Commence by recording the aspects for which you are thankful, or make use of a pre-designed journal such as the Five Minute Journal, to chronicle your daily experiences and reflect upon the emotions they evoke. Engaging in activities that promote introspection can facilitate the process of establishing a connection with oneself.

6. ASK APPROPRIATE QUESTIONS

The inquiries that individuals regularly pose to themselves often dictate the caliber of their lives. When one poses a debilitating inquiry such as, "Why do I consistently encounter these situations?", their cognitive processes engage in a quest for an explanation. The subliminal mind might even fabricate a response to such query, such as, "This occurs due to insufficient capabilities," or "This is attributed to insufficient intelligence."

Engaging in such pessimistic self-talk will only serve to heighten the challenges associated with rediscovering your true essence. Alternatively, you may contemplate inquiries such as, "In what manner may I utilize this encounter to cultivate a heightened sense of self-esteem?" In response, your mind shall actively search for solutions, often yielding an answer that not only elevates your emotional state, but also enables you to commemorate and reestablish a genuine connection with your inherent nature.

Hence, it is imperative to direct one's attention towards the formulation of high-quality inquiries. Given that posing insightful inquiries fosters an improved quality of life.

They steer our cognitive attention, exerting an impact on our cognition and emotions. The crucial aspect is to engage in a process of introspection by posing a sequence of inquiries that will enable the realization of your authentic essence. Direct your focus, exemplifying quality concerns such as:

• Which components of my life currently contribute to my utmost happiness?
• What is currently most invigorating me in my existence?

- What is the accomplishment that currently fills me with the greatest sense of pride in my life?
- At present, what is the aspect of my life that elicits the highest degree of gratitude from me?
- What is currently the primary focus of my interest in life?
- To what is my present life being devoted? • To what do I presently commit my life? • What is the current focus of my life's dedication? • Upon what does my life presently center?
- Towards whom do my affections lie?

Engaging in the regular practice of formulating high-quality inquiries will afford you the opportunity to access your most empowering emotional states. Moreover, as you persist in honing this skill, you will cultivate cognitive pathways leading to elevated levels of happiness, exhilaration, self-esteem, appreciation, bliss, dedication, and affection.

How To Set And Maintain Appropriate Boundaries

Recognize Yourself.

Gaining insight into one's thoughts, needs, habits, preferences, aversions, values, and emotional responses facilitates an enhanced understanding of one's identity. Having a clear understanding of your own identity, aspirations, and personal limits can facilitate the development of constructive interpersonal connections with others.

One can acquire the ability to effectively handle emotionally taxing and demanding circumstances through recognizing and acknowledging their presence. Grant yourself permission to release anything that no longer fulfills its purpose in your life.

Here are some situations that can evoke emotional fatigue or induce stress:

Being in the presence of an individual who exudes pessimistic vibes, engages in psychological manipulation, issues threats, places blame, engages in bullying behavior, or displays anger

Experiencing a significant life change, such as the unfortunate passing of a dear one, migrating to a different residence, facing unemployment, or undergoing a divorce, can bring about impractical demands to fulfill another person's desires.

Experiencing a sense of accountability for the emotional well-being of others.

Holding the belief that the conduct of others has an impact on one's well-being.

Due to a fear of relinquishing affection, you exhibit reluctance in expressing your needs, potentially stemming from a childhood where deviating from expected behavior resulted in disapproval.

Experiencing a sense of duty towards the well-being of others.

Recognize your own proclivities.

Regrettably, the majority of individuals succumb to the bondage of their habitual patterns. Over an extensive duration, it can be inferred that this storyline permeated our existence. It is customary to behave in specific circumstances. In order to overcome a habit, it is essential to develop an understanding of your behavioral tendencies and automatic responses, thereby actively depriving them of any sustenance.

As a result of the circumstances surrounding the Covid outbreak, my father has elected to reside in my home. From his earliest years, my Father has exhibited a discerning palate, gravitating towards meat-based or lusciously creamy dairy-based meals. Nevertheless, the recipes and photographs that I have shared serve as proof that my culinary creations are indeed the antithesis of that perception.

Consequently, subsequent to our relocation, there has been a significant modification required in my father's dietary regimen.

We minimize the significance of the alteration and his accomplishment of shedding a few undesirable pounds through this dietary approach, however, he does occasionally express dissatisfaction or register a complaint regarding the need to consume a substantial amount of vegetables. At that moment, my established tendency to seek approval from him is triggered, and I instinctively respond by becoming defensive, creating a palpable atmosphere of unease within the room.

I acknowledged my responsibility in this matter and communicated to him that, although we would persist in maintaining a nutritious diet, it constituted a considerable alteration for him. We have made the decision to either prepare or purchase a meal on a weekly basis. If he had his preference, he would cease his disparagement of our meals. This consensus has provided him with a source of anticipation while concurrently aiding in the resolution of the issue.

This opportunity allowed me to introspect and gain insights from an alternative perspective, enabling me to cultivate a non-personal reaction.

In cases of persistent problems, it is imperative to ascertain the underlying cause and acknowledge your involvement in them (as we all have a part to play), along with discerning the recurring pattern. At this juncture, acquiring the ability to "address your mistakes promptly" is of utmost importance. In that case, it is essential for you to grant yourself forgiveness.

Portia Nelson's autobiographical work titled "My Autobiography in Five Short Paragraphs" immediately springs to my thoughts. Achieving a clear perspective necessitates the cultivation of self-awareness, embracing personal accountability, and actively choosing to adopt wholesome adjustments so as to liberate ourselves from detrimental habits.

Chapter 4
Transitioning from Suffering to Empowerment
By Chidima Anusiem

B
Being deeply enamored is an exquisite sensation, and when it envelops one's being, the world appears more enchanting than ever before. The profound and ineffable dance that ensues between two individuals who share a deep affection for one another occurs sparingly throughout a person's existence, and is highly desired by countless individuals. What transpires when the bonds of affection ensnare you with an incompatible individual, and

emancipation evolves into the paramount struggle of your existence?

Allow us to commence my expedition through this ubiquitous occurrence and unearth the seven valuable insights I acquired on transcending adversity, towards empowerment.

Conclusion of an Affair during the Summer Season

The summer of 2010 had reached its conclusion. The cool autumn breeze was beginning to establish itself, and the longing for finding solace was on my mind. At the time, I was 28 years of age and not married. After an extended period of offering supplications for a life partner, it appeared improbable that the institution of matrimony would ever materialize for me. I observed the gradual diminishment of my circle of acquaintances who were unattached, as they consecutively entered into matrimony.

"Please God!" I cried. I am nearing the age of 30 and find myself in a perpetual state of solitude, questioning the aspects of my life that may require improvement. What factors could potentially be hindering my chances of forming a romantic partnership?

I experienced a profound sense of apprehension in my heart, entertaining the notion that perhaps it was not part of God's divine scheme for me to enter into marriage. Should this indeed be the situation, I merely required Him to communicate it to me promptly.

Have you ever experienced a possible correlation between your actions and the lack of response to your prayers? It appears that you may be engaged in a deeply troubling behavior of which you are unaware, but it is known to God, and He is expressing displeasure towards you due to this.

This marks the location where I found myself situated in the year of 2010. As a person of faith, I diligently devoted myself to various endeavors in order to adequately prepare for marriage, including extensively studying books on marital relationships, seeking wisdom from experienced couples, striving for personal growth, and pursuing other similar pursuits. However, it appeared that my efforts fell short despite my unwavering commitment.

Notwithstanding my increasing unease, circumstances ultimately took a favorable turn for me. During that very autumn, I was acquainted with him through a mutual acquaintance in our families. He was a resident of Florida during that period, while I was domiciled in Georgia. In our initial discourse, it became apparent that he possessed a distinct demeanor. He possessed an enchanting vocal quality, an infectious laughter, and an alluring wit. I instantly recognized that he was the ideal candidate. I experienced a rapid increase in heart rate due to intense excitement, as I perceived it as divine intervention in response to my prayers.

Following our preliminary discussion, we diligently utilized all available means of communication, including phone calls, video chats, and texting, during our spare time. I had developed a dependency on him. He was the fulfillment of numerous years of devout supplication." "He was the long-awaited response to many years of reverential entreaty." "He was the resolution to years of spiritual devotion and entreaty. His presence brought forth immense happiness and served as the catalyst that propelled me through the hours of my day. In the event that a text message or phone call was not received from him within a period of 24 hours, I experienced a state of distress. I was in constant need of his presence, requiring it on a daily, hourly, and perpetual basis. He was the one I loved dearly, my addictive obsession.

As the passing of time transformed days into weeks, and weeks into months, our love evolved with an expeditious and steadfast nature. It bore resemblance to a whimsical narrative from folklore. I used to frequently journey to Florida in order to visit him, relishing in picturesque strolls along the shoreline while he serenaded and pampered me, thus captivating my affections. He was an outstanding individual: considerate, intelligent, benevolent, pious—a complete embodiment of virtue. Moreover, the undeniable chemistry between us was astonishing. Our connection was so intense that physical affection became irresistibly constant. It became clear that we had to expedite our marriage due to the unbearable anguish of being apart.

Following a year-long courtship, we became betrothed, and solemnized our marriage a mere 10 months thereafter. However, it was within the institution of matrimony that our authentic personalities and the genuine essence of our partnership were brought to light.

CHAPTER SEVEN
Ad-dress your dressing.

The way you present yourself through your attire can either accurately or inaccurately represent your true self to others. While it is essential to possess inner beauty, it is equally imperative to cultivate an external beauty. As the saying goes, "First impressions leave a lasting impact."

When I encounter someone for the initial time, the manner in which they are attired conveys significant information about their character and personality, in my perception. Do you desire to appeal to your ideal life partner? You should be formally dressed at all times, except when you are in your private quarters.

Prior to meeting my spouse, I refrained from adorning myself with jewelry or indulging in cosmetic enhancements. One day, one of my aunts directed her attention towards me and inquired about my choice to not wear earrings. I responded by simply stating that I did not have a particular desire to wear them, with no specific reason behind it. It was at that moment that she made a rather noteworthy remark, questioning my decision by saying, "Bukky, why do you abstain from adorning earrings? It is possible that it could hinder your prospects of finding a life partner." Funny right?

Although her remark was made in jest, it has remained etched in my memory ever since. When she uttered her words, it felt as though a tremendous force struck my head, jolting me awake. Allow me to clarify, I am not insinuating that abstaining from wearing earrings obstructs the arrival of one's ideal partner; however, in my case, it seemed as though a higher power was communicating with me through this incident. Curiously enough, it is worth noting that my aunt, who imparted this message, had not yet experienced a spiritual transformation during that particular period. I perceived an additional auditory presence within my consciousness, prompting me to commence the subsequent day.

I had always harbored the desire to adorn myself with jewelries. Indeed, I hold great admiration for those who elegantly don such embellishments. However, a lingering notion within my mind continuously reminded me of its perceived sinful nature. This notion may have stemmed from the teachings of my church during my conversion to Christianity as an adolescent, encompassing the belief that wearing jewelries equated to a transgression and symbolized servitude. Nevertheless, upon thorough examination of the Scriptures, I found no evidence supporting such a proclamation.

Despite my awareness of the truth, I remained constrained by the prevailing stronghold within my psyche. On that particular day, it was in a state of disrepair.

There are certain exceptions that should be noted in such circumstances. If one receives explicit instructions from a divine entity to refrain from adorning oneself with jewelry or makeup, or even to avoid altering the natural state of one's hair, then it is deemed acceptable to comply with these directives. However, it is important not to impose these beliefs onto others or pass judgment on those who choose to engage in such practices, branding them as outcasts or transgressors. That can be referred to as self-righteousness, which is considered a transgression. Additionally, it implies that you are interfering with their autonomy, an act that is displeasing to God.

"Strategies for Attracting an Ideal Life Partner

Luckily for me, my ideal partner, despite being a pastor, has a fondness for elegant attire. Prior to our initial encounter on Facebook, we had crossed paths on two occasions, during which I abstained from adorning myself with cosmetic enhancements or accessories. His gaze remained unaffected by my lack of earrings and specific attire, displaying no signs of additional attention directed towards me. Upon encountering me on Facebook after the lapse of two years, the extent of my transformation was such that he failed to recognize my identity, despite my engagement in the very prayer that I had previously discussed. Upon learning that I was the individual in question, he experienced a profound sense of astonishment. During a conversation, he relayed to me that had I not adorned those exquisite jewelries and presented myself in such a captivating manner, the notion of considering me as a potential spouse would not have occurred to him. I inquire as to why this is the case. Individuals of the male gender are emotionally influenced by the sensory perception of visual stimuli, which encompasses the presence of esteemed individuals.

Engaging in personal grooming, such as applying cosmetics, styling one's hair, and presenting oneself in an immaculate manner, can be considered advantageous professionally and is not morally reprehensible if done in moderation. Kindly consider applying fragrance as a means of personal grooming, as it is not regarded as inappropriate. In encounters with fellow Christians, it can be challenging to endure extended periods of proximity without having to frequently seek respite for the sake of maintaining a pleasant ambiance due to unpleasant body odors.

All individuals possess a distinct odor, however, if proper hygiene practices are not adhered to, this scent can deteriorate into a particularly unpleasant state, particularly when perspiring. While it is possible that you do not possess body odor, it would be favorable for you to emanate a pleasant fragrance. Consider purchasing body spray as an investment, but kindly refrain from utilizing antiperspirants as they may have adverse effects on your well-being.

Adorn yourself in well-fitted garments that complement your physique. I am not referring to extremely short skirts or overly snug pants that accentuate every curve of your figure. Engaging in such attire may inadvertently invite unwelcome attention. If you are a woman with a larger body size, opting for oversized dresses may not be the most flattering choice. However, if you have a slender figure, such dresses can complement your body shape. Nevertheless, it is still important to maintain modesty in your attire.

Please access the internet and browse through a selection of elegant dresses, as well as explore techniques on effectively coordinating different colors. Familiarize yourself with the hairstyles that complement your features and make a habit of consistently adorning those styles. If you possess the inclination for celestial beings to meticulously adorn your hair each and every evening, it is reason enough to wear a smile. Utilize hairpieces and acquire expertise in proficient haircare for such hair. If you are familiar with the subject at hand, then you understand.

In the church, there exist a group of unmarried Christian women who currently lack any potential suitors due to their spouses diverting their attention elsewhere, potentially as a consequence of their sartorial choices.

How to Attract an Ideal Life Partner

In a formal tone, it could be expressed as follows: On a previous occasion, I offered guidance to an acquaintance recommending the application of merely lip-gloss and a high-quality face powder. However, she deemed my counsel to be overly indulgent. It is noteworthy to mention that she remains unmarried to this day, and each subsequent encounter reveals an apparent aging beyond her years.

Improve your appearance by seeking professional dental care to address any discoloration caused by neglect, thereby whitening your teeth. If one is experiencing body odor, it is advisable to seek a resolution for this issue (by increasing frequency of bathing, refraining from wearing the same clothing consecutively, and utilizing a high-quality fragrance). Please ensure you prioritize self-care. For individuals of shorter stature, it is advisable to consider the potential benefits of wearing high-heeled footwear, alongside maintaining a nutritious diet, engaging in regular physical activity, and implementing an effective skincare routine in order to enhance one's overall appearance and boost self-confidence. Look radiant always.

Furthermore, I would like to emphasize that the term "enhancements" in this context does not refer to the augmentation of breasts or buttocks. It is important to note that engaging in such procedures often leads to subsequent consequences that are more adverse than the initial condition. If you possess a small bust, please refrain from harboring distressing thoughts; rest assured that your future partner will undoubtedly find you appealing in this regard. It suits you ok? Practice self-love and prioritize your personal well-being.

Chapter 1
Guidelines for achieving success in the dating realm

The individual who will persistently remain present, and whose presence is unnecessary. Isn't it a pleasing paradox when it comes to fruition?

He is the individual from whom you cannot free yourself. The individual who remains in close proximity for extended periods of time, spanning months or even years, throughout which no notable occurrences materialize, yet he remains unperturbed by this outcome. He possesses the understanding that companionship can spontaneously arise, but he desires to remain in close proximity and remain devoted.

You are the one issuing instructions, while he is the one acquiescing. You are actively attempting to minimize contact with him, whereas he is willing to exercise patience regardless of the duration.

You have the freedom to manipulate his position as per his preference. He would not be concerned about letting you determine everything because the decision is entirely up to you. He assumes his position with a contented aura, reveling in the fact that he is crucial to the essence of your existence.

Keeping up with the evolving dating landscape, characterized by the rise of dating apps and technological advancements, presents a considerable challenge. While various core aspects of dating have largely endured, there have been notable transformations in many dating conventions. The subsequent points outline ten strategies for achieving complete mastery in the realm of dating, serving as an ultimate guide.

CHAPTER ONE
Strictly Abiding by Our Security Protocols
Maintaining certain mental safeguards is one of the fundamental methods we employ to ensure our well-being. These protective measures stem from the adjustments we have made in response to challenging circumstances, often at an early stage in our lives. As Dr. Firestone composed. This process [of developing defense mechanisms] initiates prior to our entrance into the realm of dating, originating in our formative years where detrimental interactions and influences prompt us to construct barriers or perceive the world through a restrictive

lens, thereby exerting a detrimental impact on us during adulthood. These transformations have the potential to cause a gradual inclination towards being defensive and closed-off."

The detrimental experiences we encountered during our formative years may have fostered a heightened state of caution, limiting our capacity to easily place trust in others, and instilling the expectation that individuals ought to conform to certain behavioral norms in interpersonal relationships. It is reasonable to anticipate that potential accomplices may exhibit characteristics of dishonesty, volatility, or disinterest, as our initial protectors proved to be unreliable, affected, or dismissive. Alternatively, we could expect individuals to exhibit demanding behavior, intrusive tendencies, or display a high level of dependency due to having been raised by a parent who possessed controlling, disrespectful, or materially insatiable qualities. Consequently, we create impediments that surround us, eliciting feelings of self-protection (e.g., "you don't need anyone else anyhow") or self-judgment (e.g., "there is something wrong with you that needs fixing if you desire someone to love you"). The guards that emanate from past experiences, stretching beyond our imagination, have the potential to prompt us to appear distant, undependable, or fundamentally alien to our true selves when engaging in genuine relationships.

Following Unfortunate Attractions

When individuals act upon their precautions, they frequently opt for unsuitable life partners. It may appear peculiar, nevertheless, a substantial number of individuals are unknowingly inclined towards perpetuating and duplicating negative patterns and dynamics from the past. Therefore, we may be inclined towards individuals who possess qualities similar to those of individuals within our realm of past encounters. For example, we may feel drawn to an individual who is not genuinely reachable or find ourselves feeling particularly enlightened in the presence of someone who assumes control and aggressively pursues us.

It is crucial to acknowledge that these underlying temptations are not generally aligned with our best interests and will not consistently result in stable, affectionate relationships in the long run. For instance, if we were to consider that maintaining a state of tranquility and detachment served as a means of protection employed to fulfill our specific familial needs, we might experience a sudden sense of connection or resonance with an individual who is proactive and influential in orchestrating events. However, in the context of seeking long-lasting love, this dynamic may prove limiting in the long run. We may gradually retreat into seclusion, while our collaborator gains increasingly dominant control over the life we collectively inhabit. In due course, we might find ourselves experiencing a sense of disorientation or frustration within the confines of the relationship.

3. Unleashing Your Authentic Feminine Essence

Awakening your authentic feminine identity entails becoming at ease with embracing and embodying your complete feminine essence. The feminine essence encompasses the recognition and reverence for the inherent biological distinctions between men and women, resulting in divergent modes of expressing emotions, desires, and necessities. As you embrace and embody your feminine essence in harmony, you cultivate a sense of whimsical transcendence that empowers you as a woman.

To obtain further insights on the variances between males and females concerning relationships and affection, please refer to section 8. The scientific explanation behind the phenomenon of romantic relationships between individuals of different genders.

Presently, albeit the absence of universally applicable principles governing physical allure, individuals of both genders are innately inclined towards individuals exhibiting qualities deemed attractive. This is firmly rooted in the genetic makeup of both men and women.

Based on the principles of evolutionary psychology, it can be posited that males exhibit a propensity to value the inherent genetic quality of a prospective female partner, as this could lead to offspring with enhanced physical strength and optimal health. It is necessary to acknowledge the reality that men tend to place importance on physical attractiveness, while women tend to have a preference for men who exhibit height, broad shoulders, a narrow waist, and minimal abdominal fat.

I do not infer that your undivided attention must solely focus on your appearance. Nevertheless, it is crucial to bear this aspect in consideration when aiming to allure your prospective partner.

I would propose that enhancing your overall allure (both physically and emotionally) represents the most effective approach for fortifying your prospects of captivating a suitable partner. This will unveil your authentic feminine essence and serve as your magnetic force of allure.

The Looks Versus Attractiveness!

The perception of aesthetics is inherently subjective, with attractiveness being contingent upon cultural norms, personal beliefs, and even prevailing fashion trends. Nevertheless, possessing an affable demeanor, displaying appropriate etiquette, maintaining impeccable grooming, and exuding self-assurance undoubtedly make you a strong contender for being deemed highly appealing to the majority.

I contend that the majority of individuals seek not merely physical beauty, but a sense of allure. That is a matter that can be modified and enhanced. It is imperative to grasp the significance of this, as it is the factor that will distinguish you from the archetype of a beauty pageant contestant.

Enhancing oneself is not contingent upon the opinions of others. Your enhancements should derive from the core of your being. Remain true to your authentic self and exhibit sincerity in your interactions with others.

Indeed, the significance of cultivating a dreamy disposition is not to be underestimated, as it is contingent upon one's innate inclinations, prevailing circumstances, and personal predilections. Your character serves as the bedrock of your allure.

It is imperative to bear in mind that a woman who possesses empowerment is in congruence with her authentic feminine essence.

www.ingramcontent.com/pod-product-compliance
Lightning Source LLC
Chambersburg PA
CBHW050250120526
44590CB00016B/2290